Yorkshire Terrier

By Muriel P. Lee

D1011492

BREEDERS' BEST
A KENNEL CLUB BOOK™

YORKSHIRE TERRIER

ISBN: 1-59378-910-6

Copyright © 2004

Kennel Club Books, LLC
308 Main Street, Allenhurst, NJ 07711 USA
Printed in South Korea

PHOTOS BY:
Isabelle Français,
Carol Ann Johnson
and Bernd Brinkmann.

DRAWINGS BY:
Yolyanko el Habanero.

Contents

CHAPTER 1

Meet the Yorkshire Terrier

Are you looking for a dog that weighs only a few pounds but has the spirit of a much bigger terrier? If so, the Yorkshire Terrier, or Yorkie, may be just the dog for you! Despite his diminutive size, this is a lively, plucky dog who thinks that he is much larger than he actually is and, when necessary, is able to hold his own.

The background of the Yorkie dates back to the 18th century when, during the Industrial Revolution in England, many

The Yorkshire Terrier, or "Yorkie," is a plucky toy terrier with roots in industrial England and today is one of the AKC's top ten breeds in popularity.

Scotsmen left their country and headed south, looking for work in the mills in England. Not only did these men bring their families but they also brought their dogs, which included Skye Terriers, Paisley Terriers and Clydesdale Terriers. Although these breeds ranged in size from 6 pounds to nearly 20 pounds, all were fairly heavily coated, some with a silky texture, and all carried blue-tan or gray coat colors.

The Silky Terrier resulted from crosses between the Yorkie and the Australian Terrier (below). The Silky's blue and tan coat is long but does not reach the floor.

A common breed in Yorkshire, England at the time was the Waterside Terrier, a blue-gray dog with a long coat whose size was anywhere between 6 and 20 pounds. It was a combination of these four breeds that formed the present-day Yorkshire Terrier, the beautiful long-coated dog with the

Blue and tan is one of the Australian Terier's recognized colors. This smalll member of the Terrier Group has a harsh-textured coat typical of many terriers.

silky steel blue and tan coat, prized as one of the smallest dogs in the world and the most popular toy breed on the planet.

The breeders of these dogs, mostly weavers who worked in the mills, liked to have a tough dog that could kill a rat as quickly as a terrier, but one that was small enough to carry in their pockets when they took their dogs to the pit for rat-killing competitions. Thus they desired not only the small size of the breed but also the toughness and intelligence of the terrier.

By the early 1850s, Yorkies were being shown in England in classes of Broken-haired Scotch, Scotch Terriers, Blue and Fawn Terriers or Yorkshire Terriers. The weight for these dogs fell anywhere between 5 and 18 pounds. The English Kennel Club divided the breeds that they had approved at the time into two groups—the Sporting Group and the Non-Sporting Group. The Yorkshire breed found its place in the Non-Sporting Group, but the dogs were still shown in the various classes of Scotch Terriers, Blue and Fawn Terriers and whatever other classes the dog seemed to fit. By 1886, the English Kennel Club recognized the breed as the Yorkshire Terrier and placed it in the newly formed Toy Group. The breed was able to win the Challenge Certificates that were required for dogs to become English champions. In 1898 the Yorkshire Terrier Club (of England) was formed and the breed continued to climb in popularity. Currently the Yorkie reigns in the top ten breeds in popularity in Britain.

In England, early supporters were numerous, and the breed quickly became known. In the late 1860s, Huddersfield Ben, bred by Mr. Eastwood of Huddersfield and owned by J. Forster, was shown and won nearly 75 prizes at shows. He eventually became known as the "Father of the Yorkshire

Terrier" and sired numerous champions for other kennels.

The first Yorkie whelped in the United States was recorded in 1872, only about a decade later than the breed's intro-

duction to show rings in England. Classes were first offered for the Yorkshire Terrier at American shows in 1887. The breed classes were divided by weight: under 5 pounds and

National Specialty winner Ch. Turyanne Mischief Maker, owned by Rick Krieger, aptly illustrates why the Yorkie is considered as one of the most beautiful breeds of dog.

over 5 pounds. It was soon decided, since the larger weight class had few entries, to have one weight class for all Yorkies, specifying weight range between 3 and 7 pounds. Today, the American Kennel Club breed standard limits Yorkies at 7 pounds.

The Yorkshire Terrier Club of America was formed in 1951. Among the club's many activities, it publishes a quarterly magazine and maintains a website that offers a substantial amount of information on the breed and the club itself. The club's purpose is to safeguard and promote the Yorkshire Terrier in the US through ethical breeding practices and responsible ownership.

The Yorkshire Terrier is a very popular breed in the United States, and there have been a number of very active breeders producing fine specimens. Two breeders who raised and showed excellent Yorkies in the 1950s, 1960s and 1970s were the sisters Joan Gordon and Janet Bennett of the Wildweir Kennels. Their English import Ch. Little Sir Model was the first Yorkie to win an all-breed Best in Show. Ch. Star Twilight of Clu-Mor won 26 Bests in Show and was the sire of Ch. Proud Girl of Clu-Mor, the first Yorkie bitch to win an all-breed Best in Show. Ch. Wildweir Pomp N'Circumstance sired 95 champions and was behind the bloodlines of most of the major kennels in the US. Ms. Bennet and Ms. Gordon bred or finished about 250 champions in the breed, which is a major accomplishment for any breeder in any breed.

Barbara and Ron Scott were active in the breed in the 1980s and 1990s, breeding under the Stratford prefix. Their English import Ch. Royal Icing produced 36 champions, and Ch. Stratford's Blue Max was a multiple all-breed Best-in-Show dog as well as a specialty winner. Over 60 champions were produced by this kennel. In 1978, Mrs. James Edward Clark, one of the country's most respected all-breed judges, made history by awarding Ch. Cede Higgins, owned by Charles and Barbara Switzer, Best in Show at Westminster Kennel Club. This was the first Yorkie ever to win this most prestigious of dog shows!

Many breeders and fanciers have contributed to the breed through excellent breeding and outstanding wins. At the present time, the breed places in the top ten breeds in popularity of the AKC breeds

and it has held steadfast in its ranking as number-one Toy dog in America. Through all the years, the little Yorkshire Terrier has remained a great favorite with the public.

This tiny dog is big when it comes to snuggling!

MEET THE YORKSHIRE TERRIER

Overview

- The Yorkie's beginnings can trace back to the Industrial Revolution in 18th-century England, deriving from crosses between native Scottish and English terrier breeds.
- The Yorkie's original purpose was to rid the mills of small vermin, and they were also competitors in rat-killing contests.
- It took several decades for the Yorkie to enjoy separate classification at shows and recognition as a distinct breed in its homeland.
- The Yorkie first appeared in the US in the late 1800s and has progressed to be the country's most popular toy breed.

Description of the Yorkie

Every breed of dog registered with the American Kennel Club (AKC) has an official written standard, which helps breeders and fanciers to better understand the characteristics that define the Yorkshire Terrier. The standard tells us what makes the Yorkie different from every other breed of dog. Without the breed standard, these essential characteristics could be lost. It is no accident that the Yorkie's coat is blue and tan and floor length, nor that his ears, muzzle and tail look

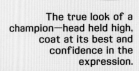

The true look of a champion—head held high, coat at its best and confidence in the expression.

a certain way. These characteristics are listed in the standard, and breeders must seek out these traits, as well as the Yorkie's typical temperament and personality, which are also described in the standard.

The Yorkshire Terrier standard has been formulated by the national breed club, the Yorkshire Terrier Club of America, and you can find the complete standard on the AKC's website (www.akc.org). The standard for the Yorkie, compared to that of other breeds, is quite short. The longest section is on the coat, which is very important for the breed. If one is going to show his Yorkie, the correct coat and color are of prime concern.

The Yorkshire Terrier is a very active, sturdy, fearless and confident terrier who is very affectionate, devoted, loyal and, of course, very loving. You will never find him boring! His bright dark button eyes

The pet trim looks a lot different from the full-length coat, but that doesn't make the dog any less of a Yorkie.

The Yorkie is a happy, friendly companion, as evidenced by this dog's smiling face.

will show that he is game for anything that you suggest. His V-shaped ears are small and carried erect. He will have a high head carriage and a confident manner, giving the appearance of great self-importance.

Even though the Yorkie is very small, he must be well proportioned and compact, with a rather short back and a level topline. His front legs should be straight and his feet round. He has a docked tail, which is carried higher than the level of the back. He must not weigh over 7 pounds at maturity if he is to be shown. However, the pet Yorkie may weigh more.

The standard describes the coat as follows: "Quality, texture and quantity of coat are of prime importance. Hair is glossy, fine and silky in texture. Coat on the body is moderately long and perfectly straight (not wavy). It may be trimmed to floor length to give ease of movement and a neater appearance if desired. The fall on the head is long, tied with one bow in center of head...or tied with two bows." It will be very difficult, and unnecessary, to keep your pet in the long coat if you are not showing him. However, even with the pet trim, he can have the cute little bow on the top of his head.

The colors of the Yorkie are basically blue and tan; however, all Yorkies are born black and change color as they mature. The standard

Standards differ from country to country, but emphasize the same trademarks that make the Yorkie the special breed that it is. This lovely show dog hails from the breed's homeland, England.

notes the following under color: "Blue: A dark steel-blue, not a silver-blue and not mingled with fawn, bronzy or black hair. Tan: All tan hair is darker at the roots than in the middle, shading to still lighter tan at the tips. Color on Body: The blue extends over the body from back of neck to root of tail. Hair on tail is a darker blue. Headfall: A rich golden tan, deeper in color at sides of head, at ear roots and on the muzzle, with ears a deep rich tan. Chest and legs: A bright, rich tan, not extending above the elbow on the forelegs nor above the stifle on the hind legs."

The colors are complicated and, if you are not looking for a show dog, this will not be of prime consideration for you. However, you do want a well-bred Yorkie and one that looks like a Yorkie should look!

Having done your homework and having decided that this may be the ideal dog for your family, you are now well on your way to finding a reputable and responsible breeder!

DESCRIPTION OF THE YORKIE

Overview

- A breed standard is an official written description, detailing the ideal physical characteristics, personality, movement and abilities of the breed.
- The Yorkshire Terrier Club of America is the breed's parent club in the US and the author of the AKC standard.
- The standard outlines the correct body structure and proportions in this tiny breed.
- A large section of the standard is devoted to coat and color, truly hallmarks of the Yorkie.

CHAPTER 3

Are You a Yorkie Person?

The Yorkshire Terrier is a toy breed, and you cannot ignore or forget this fact when deciding to add this breed to your household. This is a small dog and, because of its size, there will be certain factors that must be considered. Yorkies, like many of the terriers, feel that even though their bodies may be small, they are just as intimidating as 100-lb dogs and can take on anything that may cross their paths! They can be aggressive with other small pets, such as cats, gerbils and rabbits. Like all terriers, they may like to dig, have a

The Yorkie's diminutive size means that it's easy to take him wherever you go!

14

somewhat aggressive nature when needed and like to bark. In addition, typical of terriers, they are blessed with a lifespan of around 15 years, and throughout that time they can remain physically active and challenging. This is a breed that can also be manipulative; if your Yorkie becomes spoiled, he can and will run your household. If you want to have this breed as a pet, you must be aware of these Yorkie qualities. Having said this, though, there is no reason that a well-bred Yorkie, who is owned by a sensible owner who can train his dog and let the dog know who the boss is, cannot be a simply delightful companion for all of his years.

The Yorkie head is a thing of beauty with the long headfall, eyes full of life and bright, sweet expression.

Before purchasing your Yorkie, you must give some thought to the personality and characteristics of this dog to determine if this is the breed for you. Consider the following factors before making the decision to

Even a full-grown Yorkie won't overwhelm a small child. On the other hand, because of the breed's small size, Yorkies must always be treated with care by kids and adults alike. This is a toy breed, but not a toy.

adopt a Yorkie companion.

How much time do you have to devote to this dog? Yorkies are indeed "little people" and love to spend time with their owners. They, in fact, will be quite miserable if left unattended for hours on end. Your Yorkie will need care, companionship, training and grooming. This is almost like having a child, except that the dog remains childlike and will always require your care and supervision.

For the safety of the Yorkie, do you have a fenced yard? While Yorkies don't run away from home, as many breeds do, they can be easily distracted by a noisy bird or brazen squirrel across the street. Of course, given his "small-mammal" size, your fence cannot have large holes or gaps, or else your Yorkie will go headfirst through these openings. And don't forget, he may also choose to go under the fence—he is a terrier, and digging is one his many talents.

Also, think about your own dog history. Have you owned a toy dog before, or have you only owned larger breeds? The Yorkie is much different from ordinary regular-sized dogs. Your previous experience owning a small dog gives you a good idea of what a dog expects from you and what you must do for your dog. Since the Yorkie is an active dog, he will need exercise and lessons in manners. This is a smart dog and needs an owner who is equally as smart as, or smarter than, he is!

Your lifestyle also plays a part in this decision. Do you have small children? Young kids are not suitable companions for the delicate Yorkie. Older children may be perfect companions, provided you have the time to teach them how to handle the dog and supervise them so that they will not mistreat this pet. The Yorkie, because of his small size, will not tolerate any mistreatment from a child.

Unlike a Labrador or a Golden Retriever, who will allow a small child to ride on his back or pull his ears or tail, the Yorkie could be severely injured if mishandled. You will have to teach your children how to behave toward and around this pet.

as a child needs it. He must be fed two times a day and exercised several times a day. He needs to be held and loved, and he will like to go for rides in the car with you. You must work with him to have an obedient dog who has good manners. Your dog should

Grooming is a big consideration with the Yorkie, especially if the owner wishes to keep the dog in full coat.

So how much time is really involved with owning a Yorkie? Having time for a dog does not mean that you cannot work and own a dog. Your pet will need quality time, though, just

have at least two good outings a day; that means a walk or a good romp in the morning and the evening. Exercise should be on-lead or in the fenced yard or other enclosed area; never let him out loose to run the neighborhood.

Most types of living accommodations will suit a Yorkie. As a small breed it does not require nearly as much space as a Labrador or Mastiff. A home with a securely fenced

Yorkies pack a lot of personality and charm into their tiny bodies. It's easy to see why many fanciers own more than one.

yard is ideal, one that gives your dog room to run and stretch his legs. And remember, it is your responsibility to keep the yard clean of feces. When walking your dog, it is essential to carry a plastic

bag or two to pick up droppings. These can be easily discarded in a handy trash receptacle on your way home.

Of course, with the Yorkie there is the noise-pollution factor. Are you willing, or able, to have a dog that tends to be a bit noisy? Will your neighbors (and other family members) tolerate this? As a responsible dog owner, it is up to you to make certain that your dog is trained not to bark needlessly. The Yorkshire Terrier can be a bit noisy and yappy, and it is not fair to your neighbors to let your dog bark endlessly.

Even though the Yorkie is small, he has a high-maintenance coat that will look desperately mangled if not kept tidy. You will have to dedicate at least a weekly grooming session to keep your blue and tan angel looking sufficiently heavenly. Saintly owners brush their Yorkies daily. Grooming is essential with this breed. If left on his own, he will have a long, sweeping coat that will become

tangled and matted in very short order. However, there is no reason to keep the dog in a long coat if he is not being shown. There are many things that can be done to have an easy keeper and there will be suggestions in the grooming chapter on how to handle the coat with a relative amount of ease.

We've discussed the smallness of the dog, his terrier disposition and his long coat. The Yorkie is also appreciated for his intelligence, his devotion to his family, his abilities for keeping watch over those aroun possessions and his livel the dog for y all you can about the breed before rushing out and buying the first puppy you see.

For more information on the Yorkshire Terrier, visit the Yorkshire Terrier Club of America's website, which is an excellent source of information. Go to www.ytca.org.

ARE YOU A YORKIE PERSON?

Overview

- Are you ready to take on a tiny dog with the personality and intelligence of a much larger breed?
- A Yorkie person is prepared to raise and train a sometimes noisy and sometimes challenging terrier.
- A Yorkie person will ensure the safety and proper handling of his tiny companion.
- A Yorkie person is ready to devote much time to grooming throughout the dog's life.
- A Yorkie person will research all aspects of the breed, the pros and the cons, before deciding that this is the dog for him.

Selecting a Yorkie Breeder

I n selecting a breed as popular as the Yorkie, you will be tempted to purchase the first blue and tan tyke you meet. If you want a Yorkie yesterday, and don't care about his pedigree or background, then, by all means, run out and buy the first pup you can get for a cheap price. If, however, you care about the health, temperament, appearance and longevity of your future companion, then let's approach your breeder search with the consideration and care it deserves. In the dog world, you absolutely get what you pay for. If a breeder is willing to sell you a

You'll know you've found a good breeder when her love of the Yorkie is proudly displayed.

pup for a discount, you can be certain that you'll be paying the difference over and over at the vet's office.

You are making a classy choice in opting to buy a Yorkshire Terrier. Let's not limit your possibilities before even taking the puppy home. Even if your Yorkie will only be a pet and not a show dog or competition dog, you still want to purchase a Yorkie who looks and acts like a Yorkie. Of course! Otherwise you would just go get a mixed breed from the local pound (which of course is a worthy endeavor!).

The only way to produce sound Yorkie pups is to start with top-quality parents.

When you buy your Yorkshire Terrier, you will want to buy a healthy puppy from a responsible breeder. A responsible breeder is someone who has many years' experience in the breed and has given considerable thought before breeding his bitch. He considers health problems in the breed, has ample room in his home for a litter of puppies and has the time to

Good puppies don't just sprout up in the garden! They are the result of careful breeding by dedicated breeders who love the Yorkie.

give to each and every pup. He does not breed to the dog down the block because it is easy and he wants to show his children what the miracle of birth is all about. Above all, he does not allow anyone else to sell his puppies; he insists on meeting every new owner personally and doesn't need help in this regard.

A responsible breeder is someone who is dedicated to the breed, to breeding out any faults and hereditary problems, and whose overall interest is in improving the breed. He will study pedigrees and see what the leading stud dogs are producing. To find the right stud dog for his bitch, he may fly his bitch across the country to breed to a particular stud dog or he may drive the bitch to a dog that is located a considerable distance away. He may have only one or two litters a year, which means that there may not be a puppy ready for you when you first call. Remember that Yorkie litters are among the smallest, and some dams can have only one to three puppies in a litter.

Caring for a litter is just as much work for the dam as it is for the breeder.

A good puppy may require patience on your part, so don't hurry this process.

Check out the YTCA's website for links to regional Terrier breeder will probably be someone who has been breeding for some years and someone who participates in the breed on a national level.

The breeder has provided the pups with a secure pen in which they can spend some time outdoors for early exposure to the great big world outside the whelping box.

and local Yorkshire Terrier clubs. You should be able to find one in your area, or at least in your state. The local club should be able to refer you to their member breeders in the area, and they should also be able to answer any questions that you may have.

The responsible Yorkshire He will be a member of the local Yorkshire Terrier club and will also belong to the Yorkshire Terrier Club of America. Likely, the breeder shows his own dogs in conformation classes and has a wall decorated with champion certificates from the sires and dams in his kennel. If you meet a breeder who is "not into the show thing," you probably are visiting a hobby breeder. These breeders most likely are not reliable sources for a puppy, as they do not have the experience or

and therefore is worthy of being reproduced.

The responsible breeder will show you his facility, if he has a kennel, or invite you into his home to see the puppies and meet the dam (and sire, if

The pups' first human contact is with the breeder, who gives them love and hands-on attention to foster their bond with people.

dedication to produce healthy, sound, typical puppies. Breeders who show their own dogs (or who hire handlers to show their dogs) are interested in experts' opinions other than their own. A champion dog guarantees that at least three experts agree that this dog is a superior example of the breed,

possible). The areas will be clean and smell good. The breeder will introduce you to the dam of the puppy that you are looking at and she will be clean, smell good and be groomed. The puppies will also be clean, with trimmed toenails and clean faces. The breeder may only show you one or two puppies, as he may opt not to show you the puppies that are already sold or that he is going to keep.

The breeder will also have questions for you. Have you had a dog before? How many have you had and have you ever owned a Yorkie? Did your dogs live long lives? Do you have a fenced yard? How many children do you have and what are their ages? Are you willing to spend the time in teaching your children how to treat the new family member? Have you ever done any dog training and are you willing to go to obedience classes with your dog? Are there any other pets in your household? Do not be offended by these questions. He has put a lot of effort and money into his litter, and his first priority is to place each pup in a caring and appropriate household where he will be wanted, loved and cared for.

Just as the breeder has interrogated you, it is not inappropriate for you to have a list of questions for the breeder. Breeders like to meet potential owners who are well prepared. A good breeder will be impressed and flattered that you have taken the time to be a "smart shopper."

Ask the breeder why he planned this litter. What did he set out to accomplish with this breeding? More than likely, he will tell you exactly which traits from the sire and dam he was intending to reproduce and improve. Ask to see the pedigree for the puppy so you can evaluate the puppy's background. Titles in a pedigree, such as "Ch." or "CD," indicate that relatives of the puppy have won awards in conformation shows or obedience trials. The more titles, the better! It is worth noting that the titles that are most important are on the sire and grandsire (as well as the dam and granddam). If all the titles are attached to the names of the greats and great-greats, that's not so great!

Ask about health clearances for the sire and dam. Some of the hereditary or congenital problems known in the breed are patellar luxation, open fontanelles, Legg-Calve-Perthes disease and, to a lesser extent, elongated soft palate, collapsed trachea, progressive retinal atrophy, cataracts, keratitis sicca and kidney stones. Find out what the breeder has done to avoid these in his line. Eye clearances can be registered with the Canine Eye Registration Foundation (CERF). Good breeders will gladly, in fact proudly, provide those documents.

Don't be bashful to ask about a sales contract and the price of a puppy. Most reputable breeders have a puppy sales contract that includes specific health guarantees and reasonable return policies. They should agree to accept a puppy back if things do not work out. They also should be willing, indeed anxious, to check up on the puppy's progress after he leaves for his new home and be available if you have questions or problems with the pup. You can expect to pay a dear price for all of these breeder qualities, whether you purchase a "pet-quality" Yorkie for a companion dog or one for showing. Breeders often evaluate their puppies, and those with little or no show potential are considered "pet quality" and sold for less than their "show-quality" pups. These puppies are no less healthy; they only lack certain desirable show traits.

Many breeders place their pet-quality puppies on the AKC's Indefinite Listing Privilege (ILP). This registers the pup with AKC and allows the owner to compete in some types of AKC-licensed competition (not conformation), but does not allow AKC registration of any offspring from the mature dog. The purpose of the ILP is to prevent indiscriminate breeding of "pet-quality" Yorkies. The breeder, and only the breeder, can cancel the ILP if the adult dog develops into breeding quality.

If you have any doubts at all, feel free to ask for references and check with them. It's unlikely that a breeder will offer names of unhappy puppy clients, but calling other owners may make you more comfortable dealing with a particular breeder.

Listings of YTCA member breeders can be found on the YTCA website. Check also with the American Kennel Club's site. Their website (www.akc.org) also offers links to Yorkie breed clubs and breeders throughout the United States. Call and ask about their litters. Any information gleaned from these conversations will make you a smarter shopper when you visit a litter of pups.

SELECTING A YORKIE BREEDER

Overview

- In a popular breed, breeders abound! Reputable breeders, however, will require more research and patience to find, and this is the only puppy source you should consider.
- A responsible breeder is experienced and knowledgeable about the Yorkie, dedicated to improving the breed with every litter.
- Membership in the YTCA is a good sign, as member breeders must uphold a strict code of ethics in their breeding programs.
- Have many questions prepared for the breeder and be ready for him to interview you as well.
- Investigate the background of your potential pup and his parents. Look at pedigrees and ask to see documentation of health clearances on the parents and also the pups, where applicable.

Finding the Right Puppy

Can you imagine how such a tiny pup can make such a huge impact on your life? Are you ready?

Your quest for the perfect Yorkie, whether for pet or show, must be fueled by knowledge and regulated by patience. Although you will pay more for a show-quality Yorkie, you can expect to pay a dear price for a pet as well. Puppies are in high demand, and the top breeders receive top dollar for their dogs.

Before seeing the breeder and his pups, you should give some consideration as to whether you prefer to have a male or a female for a pet. Some individuals consider males easier to train but the more aggressive of the two sexes. Others prefer the softer disposition of a female. There are several points that should be considered in making your decision. In the Yorkshire Terrier, the size of either sex will make little difference. Yorkies basically weigh between 3 and 7 pounds as adults. A pet Yorkie may weigh 8 pounds or maybe 9 pounds, but not much more. By the way, there is no such thing as a "Teacup Yorkie." The breed comes in one size, and you're wise to avoid any breeder who's peddling Teacups.

When one Yorkie puppy is as darling as the next, how will you choose?

If you do not plan to neuter or spay your pet, the females will come into season approximately every six months. Many breeders will require you to neuter/spay your pet dog or bitch for health reasons. A bitch's season can be a difficult time for up to three weeks, as it is fairly messy and hard on the house, and will attract any loose males in the neighborhood, who will sit on your

The Yorkie is a wonderfully adaptable Toy terrier who makes a great companion for almost anyone—people of all ages, lifestyles and living situations.

doorstep like lovelorn swains. Males who are not neutered can be more aggressive and will have more of a tendency to lift their legs and to mount your leg or the furniture.

If you are not sure which sex you want, discuss it with the breeder and he will be able to give you some direction. In some cases, you may not have the liberty to select a sex, as there may only be one sex available. Often breeders keep bitches and sell dogs, though this depends on the breeder's program and philosophy. Your intentions for the puppy can play a large part in your selection of sex. If you are considering showing the Yorkshire Terrier, a male is the better choice, as they typically have fuller coats and more presence in the ring. If you are looking for a dog to breed, a female is the obvious choice, though this is not a hobby to be taken lightly.

Most likely, the breeder only has one or two puppies available, given the fact that most dams only have litters of about three pups. If you have selected your breeder with care, your choice is not going to be daunting, as it might be if you were picking a Greyhound or Great Dane puppy from a clan of ten or more in various colors and patterns. Yorkie owners have but one choice for coat color.

Even if there are only one or two puppies from which to choose, you still must consider the temperament of the puppies. Do not pick the puppy that hangs back or the one that presents himself as a whirling dervish in blue and tan. An active puppy is a good thing, though a hyper puppy can turn into a hyper adult and will require more patience and time in training. Ideally, you will find a middle-of-the-road puppy, the one that is interested, comes up to you, listens when you speak and looks very alert. You can afford to be selective, if you have patience. Don't forget—

you are adding a new member to your family and you want one that is bright, healthy and, of course, fun!

If you are a first-time puppy owner, do know that there will expenses should be less than those for a large breed, which require giant equipment and tons of kibble. Even so, grooming tools for a Yorkie will be considerably more

Spend time with the puppy and the mother of the litter. Note their reactions to each other, to you and to the breeder to gain valuable insight about their temperaments.

be expenses in addition to the price of the puppy. You will need a collar and a leash, dog dishes, food and grooming utensils, and that's just a partial list! A dog crate is really essential, as well as a fence around your yard or possibly a small fenced-in area or dog run. For the small Yorkie, the expensive than for the short-haired breeds for whom you only need a brush and comb. You must also consider the expense of having your dog groomed, if you choose not to do it yourself. And with every dog there is the cost of veterinary visits, flea and tick preparations, heartworm medication and other medical needs. These are all expenses of which you must be aware before bringing the puppy home.

You are now ready to select your puppy. You have decided that you are a Yorkie person, a dedicated owner who is ready to adopt a Yorkshire Terrier "child." You have the time to devote to making a Yorkie's life full and meaningful. Your entire family is ready for this new arrival into your home and lives. You have done your homework and have located a responsible breeder who has a litter available. While most dog breeders release puppies at around eight weeks of age, Yorkie breeders typically do not release puppies until they are three or four months old. Yorkie puppies are very tiny and require gentle handling and care.

Make an appointment with the breeder to meet the pups. Be courteous and prompt. You should arrive at the appointed time. The breeder will have the puppies ready for you to look at. They should be bouncy, clean and groomed. Their noses will be wet, their coats will have a glow or sheen and they will have a nice covering of flesh over their ribs. You will be ready to pick up one of these rascals and cuddle him in your arms.

Consider the puppy's coat, as this is one of the Yorkie's crowning glories. Whether you have a pet or show dog, a good coat makes all the difference. The puppy coat appears bluish-black and is flat and shiny. Do not select a fluffy coat, as this will develop into a woolly adult coat, which is not typical for the breed and not easy to care for. Fluffiness on the legs promises a cottony adult coat, so avoid such a puppy. Do not be turned away from a puppy who is not heavily coated, as often an insubstantial puppy coat grows into a perfect silky adult coat.

Remember that the puppy's

color is almost solid black, but you should be able to see some gold roots coming in. Look at the puppy's head and you should see some whiteness at the base of the hairs. Since the just starting to show signs of what he will look like as an adult. By this age, the pup likely has reached half his weight, so you can pretty well judge how big the adult will be. It is not

The litter's living quarters should be clean and cozy, with ample space for all of the pups and in an area where they will have frequent exposure to the breeder's family and their everyday routine.

adult Yorkie's face should be bright gold, you want to avoid a puppy whose face is too murky or orange and black mixed together. Some breeders recommend looking at the puppy's legs. Tan shadings on the pup's legs indicate that the adult's coloration should develop perfectly.

A three-month-old puppy is unusual for some pups to look a little longer than the standard describes for the adult's square proportions, but height will come in time. The puppy's back should be level, as any deviation in the topline likely will not improve. Show breeders want a puppy with a short loin so that the adult attains proper angulation. A puppy without good rear angulation will grow up to be high in the hindquarters, which is not desirable according to the standard.

If you are selecting for show potential, you want the Yorkie puppy to have good shoulder angulation as well. It is this angulation that gives the adult the desirable elegant head carriage, not length of neck. A long neck in a Yorkie is not desirable. The forelegs should be straight, typical of terrier construction, and the rear legs should appear parallel when viewed from behind, with moderate angulation as in front. A common problem in Yorkies is patellar luxation, or slipped kneecaps, which is caused by poor angulation in the rear.

While all of these physical traits are important for the typical Yorkie, temperament and health are equally key considerations. A Toy dog must be sweet and personable. Your puppy should appear friendly and outgoing, happy to meet you and ready for anything. Consider the personality of the dam, as this will shed some light on the future temperament of your puppy. Observe also how the puppy interacts with the breeder. You can tell a lot about both the puppy and the breeder by this relationship.

You should ask the breeder if the sire and dam of the litter have had their temperaments tested. These tests are offered by the American Temperament Test Society (ATTS). Responsible breeders will be familiar with this organization and will have had their animals tested. The breeder will show you the score sheets and you can easily determine if these dogs have the personalities you are looking for. In addition, this is an excellent indication that this is a responsible breeder.

Temperament testing by the ATTS is done on dogs that are at least 18 months of age; therefore puppies are not tested, but the sire and dam of a litter can be tested. The test is like a simulated walk through a park or a neighborhood where everyday situations are encountered. Neutral, friendly and threatening situations are encountered to see what the dog's reactions are to the various stimuli. Problems that are looked for are unprovoked aggression, panic without recovery and strong avoidance. Behavior toward strangers, reaction to auditory, visual and tactile stimuli, self-protective behavior and aggressive behavior are watched for. The dog is on a loose lead for the test, which takes about ten minutes to complete. Although Yorkies are not commonly temperament tested, over 82% of those who did participate in ATTS tests passed.

Alternatively, some breeders will have the temperaments of their puppies tested by a professional, their veterinarian

See which pup in the litter appeals to your family the most. Sometimes the perfect pup will pick you!

CHAPTER 5

or another dog breeder. They will find the high-energy pup and the pup that will be slower in responding. They will find the pup with the independent spirit and the one that will want to follow the pack. If the litter has been tested, the breeder will suggest which pup he thinks will be best for your

Temperament is gauged by, among other things, observing the pup's reaction to being picked up and handled.

family. If the litter has not been tested, you can do a few simple tests while you are sitting on the floor, playing with the pups.

Pat your leg or snap your finger and see which pup comes up to you first. Clap your hands and see if one of the litter shies away from you. See how they play with one another. Watch for the one that has the most appealing personality to you, as this will probably be the puppy that you will take home. Look for the puppy that appears to be "in the middle," not overly rambunctious, overly aggressive or submissive. You want the joyful pup, not the wild one. Spend some time selecting your puppy and, if you are hesitant, tell the breeder that you would like to go home and think over your decision. This is a major decision, as you are adding a family member who may be with you for 10 to 15 years. Be sure you get the puppy with whom you will all be happy.

Aside from buying a puppy, there is another option to Yorkie ownership—to adopt a "rescue" Yorkie. This will be a dog who, for any number of reasons, is looking for a new home. This will usually be a dog over one year of age and very often trained and house-broken. The breed rescue organization will bathe and groom the dog in addition to having a veterinarian's health certificate attesting to the good health of the dog.

Usually these dogs make marvelous pets, as they are grateful for being in a loving home. Not only do the national clubs have active rescue organizations, but the local clubs will also have groups of individuals working in this capacity. Rescue committees consist of very dedicated individuals who care deeply about the breed and work to assure that each dog will have an equal chance in life. Investigate the background of your prospective dog as much as possible. By going through the Yorkshire Terrier Club of America's rescue organization, you should be assured of getting a dog wtih whom you will be able to live. Information about Yorkie rescue can be found on the YTCA's website: www.ytca.org.

FINDING THE RIGHT PUPPY

Overview

- Once you've located a suitable breeder or two, it's time to have some fun meeting puppies.
- Male or female? Pet or show? High-activity or more mellow? Discuss what you want in a Yorkie and your future intentions for him to help the breeder help you pick your best match.
- Be prepared for the expenses of dog ownership before purchasing a pup.
- Know what to look for in a healthy pup that is sound physically and temperamentally.
- Rescuing an adult Yorkie is another option for prospective owners of the breed.

Welcoming the Yorkie

Bringing a Yorkie puppy home is not unlike bringing a baby home from the hospital. This 2-pound bundle will swiftly steal your heart and you will be anxious and proud to show off the "new baby" to the whole family. Before you bring the puppy home, you should have prepared the Yorkie's "nursery." You will select a room in the house where the Yorkie's headquarters will be. In this area, you will need to place the puppy's food and water bowls, his bed, his crate and his toy box. You will have to go to the pet

Make your pup feel at home by giving him a wire crate to call his own, complete with toys and comfy padding so he can snuggle up.

shop on a little shopping spree—any excuse to shop is welcome! Purchase good-quality supplies that will last for many years. You will need puppy food, bowls, a wire crate, a nice soft dog bed, a leash and collar, an ID tag, a brush and comb, nail clippers and some fun but safe toys.

Let's be a little more specific about this shopping list.

A Yorkie huddle! Your puppy will certainly miss the companionship of his littermates, his puppy "pack," during the first few days in his new home.

BOWLS

Pet shops sell dozens of different styles. It's going to be hard to resist those pretty ceramic or pottery bowls. These are nice for indoors. For outdoors, you may want to purchase a couple of stainless steel bowls that are easy to clean and can take the weather.

PUPPY FOOD

The breeder will advise you of the best brand to feed your Yorkie. Follow his advice and don't change the food

You don't need a large crate for your Yorkie, but you do need a sturdy one to keep him safe while traveling. The fiberglass crate shown here is preferred as a travel crate while the wire crate is better for use in the home.

A hug from a friend and a toy to chew will help your puppy settle in.

until it's time to switch to an adult food. Purchase the "small-bite" variety, which is especially designed for the smaller mouths of small breeds.

CRATE

There are a few kinds of crates on the market. Wire crates and hard plastic crates are the most common, though there are also wooden crates, fabric crates and mesh crates available. The wire crate is best for house-training and indoor use. The crate will serve the puppy not only for nighttime sleeping but also for spending time when he is unsuprevised or home alone. In very short order, your puppy will learn that the crate is his second "home," and he will feel safe and secure when he is in the crate. When the pup is left uncrated and alone, he will quickly become bored and begin to chew on furniture, corners of woodwork, whatever he can.

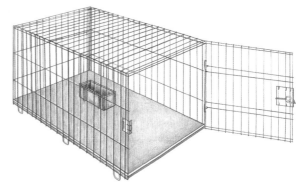

Keeping him in a confined area when you are out or cannot supervise can eliminate these problems. Be sure to add several towels or a washable blanket to the crate so that he will be comfortable. Purchase a small crate, as this will suit both the puppy and adult just fine.

A wire crate's construction provides ventilation, a clear view and a feeling of security for the Yorkie puppy.

COLLARS AND ID TAG

Your pup should have an adjustable collar that expands to fit him as he grows. Lightweight nylon adjustable collars work best for both pups and adult dogs. Put the collar on as soon as your pup comes home so he can get used to wearing it. The ID tag should have your phone number, name and address, but not the puppy's name, as that would enable a stranger to identify and call your dog. Some owners include a line that says "Dog needs medication" to hopefully speed the dog's return if he is lost or stolen. Attach the tag with an "O" ring (the kind used in key rings), as the more common "S" ring snags on carpets and comes off easily.

Today even dog collars have gone high-tech. Some come equipped with beepers and tracking devices. The most advanced pet identification tool uses a Global Positioning System and fits inside a collar or tag. When your dog leaves his programed home perimeter, the device sends a message directly to your phone or email address.

LEASHES

For your puppy's safety and your own convenience, his leash wardrobe should include at least two kinds of leads. A narrow six-foot leather leash is best for walks, puppy kindergarten, other obedience classes and leash training.

The other lead is called a "flexi" lead. This is an extendable lead that is housed in a large handle and extends and retracts with the push of a button. This is the ideal tool for exercising puppies and adult dogs and should be a staple in every puppy's wardrobe. Flexi leads are available in several lengths (8 feet to 26 feet) and strengths, depending on breed size. Longer is better, as it allows your dog to run about and check out the good sniffing areas farther away from you. They are especially handy for exercising your puppy in unfenced areas or when traveling with your dog.

GROOMING TOOLS

For the puppy coat, you will need a nice brush, with nylon

and/or natural bristles, and two metal combs, with coarse and fine teeth. A pair of scissors for trimming is good, as is a guillotine-type nail clipper. Your pet shop should sell all of these items. Depending on how much grooming you will do for your adult Yorkie, you will need to purchase additional tools. If you choose not to keep the pet Yorkie in his full-length coat, you will need an electric clippers with a medium blade.

DOG BED

Your Yorkie baby should have a bed as well as a crate. Dog beds run the gamut from small and inexpensive to elegant high-end beds suitable for the most royal of dog breeds. Of course, your Yorkie deserves the best, but you may wish to wait until he's a little older, less likely to chew it up or make a puddle on it, before you invest in the Waldorf Pooch Suite.

TOYS

It's time to play Santa Claus: bringing toys home for the Yorkie makes every day like Christmas. Puppies love to play, and Yorkies are no exception. Pet-supply stores today have whole aisles dedicated to dog toys, and

Your Yorkie pup should warm up to your family quickly. Soon he will be just like one of the kids!

some stores allow you to bring the puppy into the store to pick out his own toys. This is fun for the owner and the dog, and great socialization for the puppy. Safety, of course, is an important consideration in selecting toys, even though your puppy will only be assessing the fun factor of each toy. Yorkies are not avid chewers and will not destroy their toys too readily. Squeaky toys are popular for Yorkies and incite the breed's "give-me-a-rat" instincts. Chew toys give the puppy ample opportunities to develop his teeth and jaw bones. Always supervise your puppy whenever playing with his toys. And don't forget a nice soft toy to slip into his crate at bedtime.

BEYOND THE BASICS

Once you have the basic accessories, you are almost fully prepared for your pup's arrival. You can always visit your local pet superstore to see what other fun items you can add to your home. The pet industry is among the most inventive and resourceful, and there are always fun innovative things to try. You may also decide to purchase a baby gate or two for indoors and a good pooper scooper for the yard.

A SAFE HOME

Also before bringing your puppy into the house, you must puppy-proof it! You should be aware that a small puppy can be like a toddler and there are dangers in the household that should be eliminated. Electrical wires should be raised off the floor and hidden from view, as they are very tempting as chewable objects. Swimming pools or fish ponds can be very dangerous, so make certain that your puppy can't get into, or fall into, the water. Some barricades will be necessary to prevent an accident. Not all dogs can swim or climb out of the water. Watch your deck railings and make sure that your puppy cannot slip through the openings.

If you have young children in the house, you must see that they understand that the small puppy is a living being and must be treated gently. They cannot pull his ears, pick him up and drop him or otherwise handle him roughly. This is your responsibility. A child taught about animals at an early age can become a lifelong compassionate animal lover and owner. Use your common sense in all of these issues. Consider where a young child can get into trouble and your puppy will be right behind him!

BRINGING THE PUPPY HOME
If you are driving some distance to pick up your pet, take along a towel or two, a water pan and your leash and collar. Also take along some plastic baggies and a roll of paper towels in case there are

any potty accidents or carsickness.

When the pup comes into the house for the first time (after he has relieved himself outside), let him explore his new surroundings and give him a light meal and a bowl of water. When he is tired, take him outside again and then tuck him into his crate, either to take a nap or, hopefully, to sleep through the night.

The first day or two for your puppy should be fairly

Make sure that you are welcoming your puppy into a safe environment indoors and out. In the yard, beware of poisonous plants, gardening chemicals, mulch and fertilizers, all of which are dangerous to dogs.

CHAPTER 6

quiet. He will then have time to get used to his new home, surroundings and family members. The first night, he may cry a bit, but if you put a safe toy and small blanket in his crate, these will give him some warmth and security. A nearby ticking clock or a radio playing soft music can also be helpful. Remember, he has been uprooted from a sibling or two, his dam and his familiar breeder, and he will need a day or two to get used to his new family. If he should cry this first night, let him be and he will eventually quiet down and sleep. By the third night, he should be well settled in. Have patience and, within a week or less, it will

Your Yorkie pup doesn't need large quantities of food, but he does require top quality.

seem to you, your family and your puppy that you have all been together for years.

FEEDING THE PUPPY

Nutrition for your puppy is actually very easy. Dog-food companies hire many scientists and spend millions of dollars on research to determine what will be a healthy diet for your dog. Your breeder should have been feeding a premium small-breed puppy food and you should continue on with the same brand. As the dog matures, you will change over to the adult formula of the same dog-food brand. Do not add vitamins or anything else unless your veterinarian suggests that you do so. Do not think that, by cooking up a special diet, you will turn out a product that will be more nutritional than what the dog-food companies are providing.

Your young puppy will probably be fed three times a

day and perhaps as many as four times a day. As he starts growing, you will cut his meals to two times a day, in the morning and in the evening. By the time he reaches eight months of age, you will be changing over to the adult-formula food. You can check the dog-food bag for the amount, per pound of weight, that you should be feeding your dog. To the dry kibble, you may add water to moisten and possibly a table-spoon or so of a canned brand of dog food for flavor.

Some Yorkies have delicate digestive systems, so keep this in mind when feeding the dog. Avoid table scraps and give him a dog biscuit at bedtime. Keep a good covering of flesh over the ribs but do not let your Yorkie become a fat boy! However, the more active the dog, the more calories he will need. And, always, have fresh drinking water available. This may include a bowl of water in the kitchen and another outside in the yard for time spent outdoors.

WELCOMING THE YORKIE

Overview

- Food, bowls, a crate, a collar and leash, an ID tag, grooming equipment, a dog bed and, of course, toys will be among the things that you'll need in advance of the "new baby's" arrival.
- The house must be "puppy-proofed," made free of all potential hazards indoors and out.
- Make your puppy's ride home and first few days low-key, doing what you can to help him be comfortable and get settled in.
- Take your breeder's advice on the best feeding routine and how to make changes as the pup matures.

CHAPTER 7

Getting to Know Your Yorkie Puppy

It's a huge world out there to such a small puppy. As the owner, you must help him fit into his new human pack and make him feel at home.

Your Yorkie depends on you for everything from his water and kibble to his education and good manners. Naturally, you will want to get to know your puppy, and you will do this as you socialize him, teach him his name and begin his education.

HOUSE RULES

Socializing your puppy is very important if you want a dog that fits into your home and a dog that is a good companion who is enjoyed by everyone. Socializing a puppy is similar to when you bring home a new baby. Hold and pet your puppy so that he knows that he is wanted and loved. Do not play with him constantly, as he is very young and needs time to rest up and sleep. Keep him to a schedule as much as you can, as he will become schedule-oriented very quickly. If he knows that you rise at 7:00 every morning, and shortly after you will take him outside, he will wait for you to let him out instead of relieving himself in his crate.

Let your Yorkie pup do some exploring in your fenced yard, but be sure to supervise him wherever he goes.

Habits, and that includes good and bad habits, that are learned at an early age become lifelong habits, so it is best to start out on the right foot. Don't let your puppy chew on the leg of the old kitchen table and think that it's cute, because before long he will have chewed on the leg of your expensive dining-room table. Set limits and make sure that the pup sticks to them.

Safe toys keep your puppy occupied while teaching him proper chewing habits.

Keep him confined to a specific area, such as the kitchen or den, until he is trained and fairly mature. Use baby gates and he will quickly learn that he is welcomed in certain areas of the house and not welcomed in other areas. And, of course, put him in his crate when you leave home, as he will be comfortable in his "house" and he will sleep until you return.

CHOOSING A NAME

One of the important factors in training a young pup is to give him a name. Sometimes it may take a week or so before you find a name that fits the dog. Other times you will have the puppy named before you bring him home. In general, short one- or two-syllable names are the easiest for training. The best name of all, of course, is Ralph, because both humans and other dogs can then call your Yorkie by name! Longer names are difficult for humans (as well as the neighborhood dogs). You don't want to have call out, "Belvidere, suppertime!" when it's so much easier to say, "Eat your din-din, Blanche."

A nice British name is perhaps the best, well befitting the Yorkie's heritage and politeness. Harry, George, William, Sarah and Geoffrey are all good choices. Whichever name you choose, use it often and always in a positive way. Never use the dog's name when you scold him, and never call a dog to you and then scold him.

PUPPY GAMES

Your goal in early training is to get your Yorkie to like you. Generally, Yorkies like people. Once you have gained your dog's trust and love, then training becomes infinitely easier. Keep your puppy's kindergarten positive and fun.

Puppy games are a great way to entertain your puppy and yourself, while sublimi-person holds and pets the pup while the other calls him: "Puppy, puppy, come!"

Creating a bond with your Yorkie as a puppy means that he will grow up to be a devoted and loving friend and companion.

nally teaching lessons in the course of having fun. Start with a game plan and a pocketful of tasty dog treats. Keep your games short so you don't push his attention span beyond normal puppy limits or tire him out too much.

Puppy Catch-Me

This game helps teach the come command. With two people sitting on the floor about 6 to 8 feet apart, one in a happy voice. When the pup comes running, reward him with big hugs and give a tasty treat. Repeat the game back and forth several times...don't overdo it.

You can add a ball or toy and toss it back and forth for the puppy to retrieve. When he picks it up, praise and hug some more, give him a goodie to release the toy, then toss it back to person number two. Repeat as described.

HIDE AND SEEK

This is another game that teaches the come exercise. Play this game outdoors in your yard or other confined safe area. When the pup is distracted, hide behind a tree or bush. Peek out to see when he discovers you are gone and comes running back to find you (trust me, he will do that). As soon as he gets close, come out, squat down with arms outstretched and call him: "Puppy, come!" This is also an excellent bonding technique and teaches the puppy to depend on you.

WHERE'S YOUR TOY?

Start by placing one of his favorite toys in plain sight. Ask your puppy "Where's your toy?" and let him take it. Repeat several times. Then place your puppy safely outside the room and place the toy where only part of it shows. Bring him back and ask the same question. Praise highly when he finds it. Repeat several times. Finally, conceal the toy completely and let your puppy sniff it out. Trust his nose...he will find his toy. Yorkie puppies love to have fun with their people. Games are excellent

All packed up and ready to go. Make your Yorkie's travel crate a comfortable place with a crate pad and a favorite toy or two.

teaching aids, and one of the best ways to say "I love you" to your puppy.

DRIVING

You should get your dog used to riding in the car at an early age. Most dogs love to go for rides and, if given the opportunity, they would gladly take the steering wheel! Teach him some car manners, such as no riding on the driver's lap, no racing about the car from window to window and no chewing on the arm rests.

It is also very important to remember not to take your dog out and leave him alone for even a few minutes in the car. A car can heat up very quickly, and the dog will not be able to cope with the heat.

Since you have purchased that nice shiny wire crate, it will very easily fit on your car's back seat. The safest way to travel in a car with a Yorkie is in his crate. Even though the Yorkie would rather sit on your lap or peer out of the back window, your safest option is the crate.

GETTING TO KNOW YOUR YORKIE PUPPY

Overview

- Socialization and teaching the house rules begin right away. These lead to a well-behaved, confident dog who's a pleasure to be around.
- Choose a name for your pup and use it often so that he learns that you're talking to him when you use it.
- Games with the puppy help nurture his bond with you and introduce commands in the course of fun.
- Travel safety is important; the best way for a dog to travel in the car is in his crate.

House-training Your Yorkie

Your Yorkie must be housebroken, and this job should begin as soon as you bring him home. Do not think that you can delay the task of toilet training just because you have a small dog!

Every time your puppy wakes up from a nap, he should be quickly taken outside. Watch him and praise him with "Good boy!" when he urinates or defecates. Give him a pat on the head and take him inside. He may have a few accidents but, with the appropriate "No" from you, he will quickly learn that it is better to go outside than to

You must begin house-training your Yorkie on the very first day he arrives in your home. Dogs are creatures of habit, so don't give him a few days to form a habit of "going" wherever he wants.

do his business on the kitchen floor and be scolded.

You will soon learn the habits of your dog. However, at the following times it is essential to take your Yorkie out: when he gets up in the morning, after he eats, before he goes to bed and after long naps. As he matures, he will probably only have to go out three or four times a day. Some dogs will go to the door and bark when they want to be let out and others will nervously circle around. Watch and learn from his signs.

Dog crates are a major help in housebreaking, as most dogs will not want to dirty their living quarters. Some experienced breeders insist on crate use after their puppies leave, and a few even crate-train their pups before they send them home. But it's more likely that your pup has never seen a crate, so it's up to you to make sure his introduction to the crate is a pleasant one.

With a small dog like the Yorkie, paper training is a viable option, although many feel that crate training is the most reliable way to housebreak a dog.

Those without fenced yards will need to take their Yorkies out for potty trips. With an adult, this should only be about three or four times a day. Don't forget to clean up!

Introduce the crate as soon as your pup comes home so he learns that this is his new "house." This is best accomplished with treats. For the first day or two, toss tiny treats into the crate to entice him to go in. Say the word "Crate" every time he enters it. You also can feed his first few meals inside the crate, with the door still open, so the crate association will be a happy one.

Put your Yorkie in his crate at night and close the crate door. He will sleep through the night in the crate and he will hold his bladder until he wakes up. Well, usually, but give the puppy some slack. From his very first night, your puppy should sleep in his crate…don't start on the second or third night (unless it's already the third night when you're reading this).

If your Yorkie whines when you close the crate door, do not let him out! His first lesson should not be: "If I cry, I get out." If you are a softie (and you probably are), you can place the crate next to your bed so the puppy can see you, but do not sleep next to the crate. Your presence will comfort him and you'll also know if he needs a midnight potty trip. Whatever you do, do not take the puppy into bed with you. To a dog, on the bed means equal, which is not a good idea this early on, when you are trying to establish yourself as pack leader.

During the daytime, make a practice of placing your puppy in his crate for naps, time-outs and an hour here and there when you are busy and unable to watch him closely. Not to worry…he will let you know when he wakes up and needs a potty trip. If he falls asleep under the table and wakes up when you're not there, guess what he'll do first? Make a puddle, then toddle over to say "Hi!"

In order for house-training to be effective, you have to be more aware of the dog's potty needs than he is. Dogs are creatures of habit, and predicting the next drop isn't all that difficult. Routines, consistency and an eagle eye are your keys to house-training success. Here's the basic itinerary: puppies always "go" when they wake up (quickly now!), within a few minutes after eating, after play periods and after brief periods of confinement. Most pups under 12 weeks of age will need to eliminate at least every hour or so, or around 10 times a day.

Always take the puppy outside to the same area, telling him "Outside" as you go out. Pick a "potty" command, ("Hurry up," "Go potty" and "Get busy" are the most commonly used), and use it when he does his business, lavishing on him lots of "Good puppy!" praise. Use the same exit door for these potty trips and confine puppy to the exit area so he can find it when he needs it. Watch for sniffing and circling or other signs that

signal he has to relieve himself. Don't allow him to roam the house until he's house-trained; how will he find that outside door if he's three or four rooms away?

A fun dog bed is an adorable accessory in which your Yorkie can cuddle up, but it does not take the place of a crate. The crate offers many benefits for safety and training, and is a highly recommended tool for most breeds.

Of course he will have accidents. All puppies do. If you catch him in the act, bellow "Noooooooooo," clap your hands loudly and scoop him up to go outside. Your voice should startle him and make him stop. Be sure to praise when he finishes his duty outside.

If you discover a puddle on the floor...more than three or

four seconds after the puddle was piddled…you're too late. Pups only understand in the moment and will not understand a correction given more than five seconds after the deed. Correcting any later will only cause fear and confusion for the puppy, even if it relieves your frustration. Just forget it and vow to be more vigilant.

Despite its many benefits, crate use can be abused. Puppies under 12 weeks of age should never be confined for more than two hours at a time, unless, of course, they are sleeping. A general rule of thumb is three hours maximum for a three-month-old pup, four to five hours for the four- to five-month-old and no more than six hours for dogs over six months of age. If you're unable to be home to release the dog, arrange for a relative, neighbor or dog-sitter to let him out to exercise and potty.

One final, but most important, rule of crate use:

Never, *ever*, use the crate for punishment. Successful crate use depends on your puppy's positive association with his "house." If the crate represents punishment or "bad dog stuff," he will resist using it as his safe place. Sure, you can crate your pup after he has sorted through the trash to keep him out of your way as you clean up. Just don't do it in an angry fashion or tell him "Bad dog, crate!"

If you are unable to use a crate for training, or prefer to paper-train your Yorkie puppy, the routine is basically the same. Assign an out-of-the-way elimination place (in front of the back door?) and cover it with newspaper. Take your puppy to the designated papered area on schedule. Use the specified potty word, and praise when he does his business. Do not use the area for any other purpose except potty breaks. Keep the area clean. You can place a small piece of soiled paper on the clean ones to remind puppy why he's there. His nose will tell him what to do.

If you are crate-shy, what can you do with your uncrated puppy when you're not home? Confine him to one room with baby gates or another dog-proof barrier. Puppy-proof the room by removing anything the pup could chew or damage and hurt himself within the process. But even in a stripped environment, some pups will chew through drywall if bored. An exercise pen 4 feet by 4 feet square (available through pet suppliers), sturdy enough that pup can't knock it down, will provide safe containment for short periods. Paper one area for elimination, with perhaps a blanket in the opposite corner for napping. Safe chew toys should help keep him happy while you're gone.

Housebreaking doesn't happen overnight. Be patient and remember that successful house-training revolves around consistency and repetition. Maintain a strict schedule and use your key words consistently. Well-trained owners have well-trained pups...and clean, nice-smelling houses!

HOUSE-TRAINING YOUR YORKIE

Overview

- Teaching your puppy proper toileting habits begins on day one.
- Learn to use a crate correctly, as it will be a most helpful tool for housebreaking as well as general care and safety of your Yorkie.
- Only allow positive associations with the crate.
- Take puppy out often, praising him when he "goes" in the right spot.
- Scolding for a potty accident will only be effective if you catch him in the act.
- Consistency is the key in teaching your dog to adopt the toileting routine.

CHAPTER 9

Teaching Basic Commands

Your puppy's social- ization should have begun before you bring him home. He will be used to family and strangers, and average noises in the house and outdoors will not startle him. Socialization for your puppy is very important, and good breeders will begin this with their litters. It is especially good if there are children in the breeder's family so that the pups can meet some young people.

Let your Yorkie meet the neighbors and let him play for a few minutes. Take him for short walks in public places where he will see people and other dogs as well as hear strange

Your trained Yorkie will be a well-behaved companion with whom you will love to spend time.

noises. Watch other dogs, however, as they are not always friendly. Keep your dog on leash and you will have control over him, ensuring that he stays safe and behaves politely around everyone you meet.

You will find it to your advantage to have a mannerly dog; therefore, knowledge of some basic commands will make your dog a better citizen. One of the family members should attend puppy kindergarten classes, from which all further training will grow. This is a class that accepts puppies from two to five months of age and takes about two months to complete. You will cover the basics: sit, heel, down, stay and recall (or come). There are definite advantages to each. Sit and heel are great helps when walking your dog. Who needs a puppy walking between your legs, lunging forward or lagging behind, in general acting like a nuisance? Have your dog walking like a gentleman or lady on

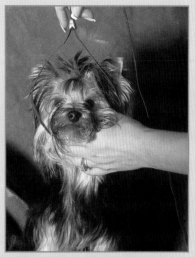

A Yorkie needs only a lightweight lead and collar, but a very thin lead like this one is designed for the show ring, not for training.

The commands have many practical uses; for example, when you need your Yorkie to stay lying down on the grooming table.

your left side and sitting as you wait to cross the street. Recall is very important if your dog either escapes from the yard or breaks his leash and you need to call him back.

Here is a short rundown of the commands. If you attend puppy classes, or obedience training classes, you will have professional help in learning these commands. However, you and your dog can learn these very basic exercises on your own.

SIT COMMAND

This is the exercise with which you should begin. Place your dog on your left side as you are standing and firmly

Your Yorkie may need a very gentle push to show him the correct sit position, but it won't take him long to get the idea.

say "Sit." As you say this, run your hand down your dog's back and gently push him into a sitting position. Praise him, hold him in this position for a few seconds, release your hand, praise him again and give him a treat. Repeat this several times a day, perhaps as many as ten times, and before long your pup will understand what you want.

STAY COMMAND

Teach your dog to stay in a seated position until you call him. Have your dog sit and, as you say "Stay," place your hand in front of his nose and take a step or two, no more at the beginning, away. After ten seconds or so, call your dog. If he gets up before the end of the command, have him sit again and repeat the stay command. When he stays until called (remembering to start with a very short period of time), praise him and give him a treat. As he learns this command, increase the space that you move away from the dog as well as the length of time that he stays.

COME COMMAND

Your Yorkie will love to come back to you when called. The idea is to invite him to return, offering a treat and giving lots of praise when he does so. It is important to teach the come command, for this should bring your dog running back to you if ever he is danger of moving out of sight.

As with all commands, keep the come exercise light and gay. This is positive training we're using here. No dog, especially one as bright as the Yorkie, will come to you if you sound as if you're not happy. Dogs respond to joy— clapping, high-pitched sounds, your elation to see them. Use this when teaching the come exercise. Your Yorkie should always think that "come" will lead to good things—never punishment or scolding.

HEEL COMMAND

Have your dog on your left side, with his leash on, and teach him to walk with you. If your pup lunges forward, give the leash a quick snap and say a firm "No." Then continue to walk your dog, praising him as he walks nicely by your side. Again, if he lunges, snap his leash quickly and say a smart "No." He will quickly learn that it is easier and more pleasant to walk by your side. Never allow him to lunge at someone passing by you.

To teach your Yorkie to stay, use your hand as a stop sign along with your verbal command "Stay."

DOWN COMMAND

This will probably be the most complicated of the basic commands to teach, as the down position is a submissive

CHAPTER 9

one. Place your dog in the sit position, kneel down next to him and place your right hand under his front legs and your left hand on his shoulders. As you say "Down," gently push his front legs out into the down position. Once you have him down, talk gently to him, stroke his back so that he will be comfortable and then praise him. With your tiny Yorkie, you may prefer to begin teaching the down on your lap or the sofa before trying it on the floor.

MORE HELPFUL COMMANDS
"Off" is an important command, as a bouncy Yorkie will become active enough to finish off the candy dish on the coffee table or jump on the new and expensive sofa. Say "Off, Tiny" and then push him down on his four feet. Again, dogs are smart, particularly Yorkies, and he will quickly learn what "Off" means.

Another good command is "Kennel up" to tell the dog to go to his crate. Along with "Kennel up" you can teach "Bedtime" for when it's time to go to his crate for the night. Do not confuse the two and tell him "Bedtime" when you are only going to the store and will be back in an hour. Dogs quickly learn that "Bedtime" means a treat and to bed for the night. "Kennel up" means that you will be back soon. And, of course, the most basic of commands is "No." Say it firmly and with conviction. Again, your dog will learn that this means to keep off, don't do it or don't even think about it.

The down exercise presents a challenge to all dog owners, as it is not a dog's favorite position to assume on command. It is best approached gently, with reassurance and, of course, treats.

A FEW MORE TIPS

In all of your commands, you must be fair (don't tell him to sit when he is already sitting), consistent (don't let him jump on the sofa sometimes and not at other times) and firm in speaking all commands. Firm, however, does not mean rough. Be positive and gentle with your tiny dog. After the dog does what you want, give him a pat on the head and praise: "Good boy!" If he has achieved some great success, give him a treat along with the praise.

A big part of training is patience, persistence and routine. Teach each command the same way every time, do not lose your patience with the dog (he will not understand) and reward him for performing his command properly. With a Yorkie, you will find that your puppy will learn these commands very quickly. You, and guests to your home, will certainly appreciate a well-behaved dog!

TEACHING BASIC COMMANDS

Overview

- Hopefully your breeder began early socialization with the litter. You will pick up where the breeder left off, introducing your pup to new people, animals, sights and sounds.
- Consider a puppy training class, which has benefits for training and socialization.
- The basic commands include sit, stay, come, heel and down. "Off," "No" and commands to tell the pup to go to his crate are also important words that your dog should understand.
- Patience, persistence, positive and practice! Remember these "Ps" of training!

Home Care for Your Yorkie

It's important to keep your Yorkie hydrated at all times, so be sure to bring along water when you travel together.

Taking care of a little dog is a big responsibility. Hardy and healthy though he is, the Yorkshire Terrier is a delicate 5-pounder. Bear in mind that because of the diminutive size of the Yorkie, the dog can sustain greater injuries than a larger dog like the Labrador Retriever from simple everyday mishaps. Watch where you sit, where you step and where you put things, and you can eliminate many of these accidents.

Once your dog is mature and remaining well, he will only need a yearly visit to the veterinary clinic for a thorough check-up and a booster shot for the vaccines. Part of the physical exam should be a full dental exam, ensuring that the teeth, gums and mouth are healthy.

The teeth deserve regular attention at home. I do not recommend use of a dental scraper by the average pet owner, as this can cause injury to a toy dog is used incorrectly. You can brush your Yorkie's teeth with a toothbrush and toothpaste made for dogs (not for humans!) and leave scraping to the vet. A crunchy dog treat every night before bedtime will also help to keep the tartar down.

Expressing the anal glands is not the greatest of tasks, besides being quite smelly. You may find that it is easier to have this done during the yearly trip to the vet. On occasion, the anal glands will become impacted, requiring veterinary attention to clean them out.

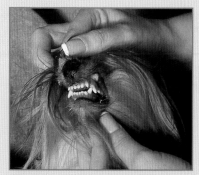

Dental care is one of the most important components of your Yorkie's home-care routine. It is important for all dogs, but even more so for toy breeds, which tend to be prone to tooth problems.

Your vet may do a thorough tooth scraping when you and your Yorkie go for his physical exam.

RECOGNIZING SYMPTOMS

By now, you know your Yorkie well. You know how much he eats and sleeps and how hard he plays. As with all of us, on occasion he may "go off his feed" or appear to be sick. If he has been nauseated for 24 to 36 hours, has had diarrhea for the same amount of time or has drunk excessive water for five or six days, a trip to the veterinarian is in order. Make your appointment and tell the receptionist why you need the appointment right away.

The veterinarian will ask you the following questions:

- When did he last eat a normal meal?
- How long has he had diarrhea or been vomiting?
- Has he eaten anything in the last 24 hours?
- Could he have eaten a toy or a piece of clothing or anything else unusual?
- Is he drinking more water than usual?

The veterinarian will check him over, take his temperature and pulse, listen to his heart, feel his stomach for any lumps, look at his gums and teeth for color and check his eyes and ears. He will probably also draw blood to run tests.

At the end of the examination, the vet will make a diagnosis and recommend treatment. He may send your dog home with you with some antibiotics, take some x-rays or keep the dog overnight for observation.

Follow your veterinarian's instructions, and you will find that very often your dog will be back to normal in a day or two. In the meantime, feed him light meals and keep him quiet, perhaps confined to his crate.

PESKY PESTS ON OUR PETS

Parasites can be a problem, and there are certain ones of which you should be aware. Heartworm can be a deadly problem and some parts of the country can be more prone to this than others. Heartworms become very massive and wrap themselves around the dog's heart. If not treated, the dog will eventually die. In the spring, call your veterinarian and ask if your dog should have a heartworm test. If so, take him to the clinic and he will be given a test to make certain that he is clear of heartworm. The vet will prescribe heartworm preventative medication. This is important, particularly if you live in areas where mosquitoes are present.

Fleas are also a problem, but particularly in the warmer parts of the country. You can purchase flea powder or a collar from the pet shop or ask your veterinarian what he suggests that you use. There are many effective spot-on treatments to control fleas, ticks and other pests. If you

There may be insects and allergens lurking among the flowers that can irritate your dog. The Yorkie's long coat may hide such problems, so get in the habit of checking your dog's skin and coat regularly.

suspect fleas, lay your dog on his side, separate the coat to the skin and see if you see any skipping, jumping or skittering around of little bugs.

Ticks are more prevalent in wooded and grassy areas. Ticks are small (to start) and dark, and they like to attach themselves to the warm parts of the ears, the leg pits, face folds, etc. The longer they are on the dog, the bigger they become, filling themselves with your pet's blood and becoming as big as a dime. Take your forceps and carefully pull the tick out to make sure you get the pincers. Promptly flush the tick down the toilet or light a match to it. Put alcohol on the wound and a dab of antibiotic salve. Let common sense and a good vet be your guide in coping with these health problems.

WEIGHT CONTROL

Your adult Yorkie should be maintained on an adult-formula dog food for small breeds. Keeping him at his proper weight is essential, as extra ounces do count in a Yorkie! Obesity is a big canine killer. If your Yorkie no longer has a "waist," cut back on portions and treats. Avoid table scraps as a rule; these cause upset tummies and some "people foods,"

including chocolate, onions, grapes, raisins and some nuts, are toxic to dogs. Encourage a "couch potato" Yorkie to be more active. Proper weight contributes to longevity and a better quality of life for your precious companion. Need we say more?

FIRST AID

Every home with a pet should have a first-aid kit. You should keep all of your first-aid items together in a box, kept in a handy place along with your vet's emergency phone number. Many of these items can be purchased very reasonably from your local drug store. Here are the items you will need:

- Cotton balls;
- Alcohol for cleaning a wound;
- Antibiotic salve for treating the wound;
- Over-the-counter eye wash in case your dog gets something in his eyes or

just needs to have his eyes cleaned;

- Forceps for pulling out wood ticks, thorns, burs and splinters;
- Styptic powder for when a toenail has been trimmed too short and bleeds;
- Triple-antibiotic cream.
- Boric acid (to soak feet, not for eye care);
- Rectal thermometer;
- A nylon stocking to be used as a muzzle if your pet should be badly injured.

Accidents can happen and, if they do, you must remain as cool, calm and collected as possible under the circumstances. You should acquaint yourself with emergency situations and their symptoms, as well as canine first-aid techniques. You want to be able to help your Yorkie as quickly as possible while contacting the veterinarian and awaiting further advice. Check and see if your breed club or local humane society offers canine first-aid seminars, which are helpful and informative for dog owners.

HOME CARE FOR YOUR YORKIE

Overview

- A tiny breed is a huge responsibility. A sturdy breed for his size, the Yorkie still is a delicate creature who must be handled with care.
- Dental care is important with toy dogs, who are prone to problems with their teeth.
- Know your dog, his behavior and his routine well. Deviations could indicate a health problem that requires veterinary attention.
- Be proactive in parasite control, both internal and external.
- Have a well-stocked canine first-aid kit as well as basic knowledge of symptoms and first-aid procedures.

CHAPTER 11

Grooming Your Yorkie

D o understand before purchasing your dog that this is a breed with a coat that needs maintenance, whether you have a dog for the show ring or one that is a household pet? Think of it in terms of your child—you bathe your youngster, comb his hair and put a clean set of clothes on him. The end product is that you have a child that smells good and looks nice, and whom you enjoy having in your company. It is the same with your dog—keep the dog brushed, clean and trimmed and you will find it a

An ideal Yorkie owner is one who enjoys spending time grooming her dog to look his beautiful best.

pleasure to be in his company. However, it will require some effort to do this.

For all his petiteness, the Yorkshire Terrier is a heavily coated breed and requires at least weekly coat care. If you are planning to show your dog, you will be ahead of the game if you purchase your puppy from a reputable breeder who grooms and shows his own dogs. If so, this is the individual to see for grooming lessons to learn how to get your dog ready for the show ring. Grooming for the show is an art, and an art that cannot be learned in a few months. Furthermore, it is very difficult but not impossible to learn it from a book.

Here are the tools that you will need if you are going to do your own grooming:

1. A grooming table, something sturdy with a rubber mat covering the top, with a grooming arm or a

You and your Yorkie will spend much time together in grooming tasks, so it's best to accustom him to the process as early as possible.

While a grooming table is a must for a full grooming session, touch-ups here and there can be done with the dog on your lap once he's accustomed to being brushed.

"hanger." (You can also use a table in your laundry room with an eye hook in the ceiling for holding the leash.) Your dog will now be comfortable even if confined and you will be

A coat conditioner is useful for detangling and also to apply before wrapping the coat to give it a nice healthy sheen.

able to work on the dog and trim his toenails with little difficulty. Grooming is a very difficult and frustrating job if you try to groom without a table and a grooming arm.

2. A wide-toothed comb and a fine-toothed comb, a natural bristle brush, a good sharp pair of scissors

Wrapping the coat should only be done by those who know the procedure; otherwise, it could damage the coat.

and a toenail trimmer.

3. A shampoo and a coat conditioner.

Set your dog on the table and put the leash around his neck. Have your leash up behind the ears and have the leash taut when you fasten it to the eye hook. Do not walk away and leave your dog unattended, as he can jump off the table and be left dangling from the leash with his feet scrambling around in the air, a dangerous situation. If your dog is cooperative, you may also lay him on his side on the table for part of the grooming.

Take your brush and brush out the entire coat.

Brush the whiskers toward the nose, the body hair toward the tail, the tail up toward the tip of the tail. Brush the leg furnishings up toward the body and brush the chest hair down toward the table. Hold the dog up by the front legs and gently brush the stomach hair, first toward the head and then back toward the rear. For cleanliness, you may want to take your scissors and trim the area around the penis. With the girls, trim some of the hair around the vulva.

Now that your dog is brushed out, comb through the coat with your metal comb. The Yorkie's coat is parted down the middle, with the coat falling down both sides. You may find some small mats, and these can be worked out with your fingers or your comb. If you brush your dog at least once a week, you will not have too much of a problem with mats. Once the coat is

TOP: Show dogs often have their coats wrapped as shown to promote growth. BOTTOM: A special "jacket" can be worn over the wrapped coat to further protect it, especially when outdoors.

completely brushed and combed through, you can take your scissors and even off the coat at floor length, "knee length" or however short you want it.

When you are finished, place your Yorkie in a

laundry tub and give him a bath, using first the shampoo and then the coat conditioner. When he has been blown dry, brushing as you dry, the coat should be combed out once more. You will have a marvelous-looking and very clean dog!

For a pet trim on the Yorkie, you will require an electric clipper with a #8 blade (medium) as well as a pair of scissors and brush. A groomer or breeder should demonstrate the pet trim once for you before you mangle your Yorkie's coat!

A metal comb ensures that the coat is free of mats and tangles.

To protect the long headfall, the hair is wrapped once the topknot is sectioned off and put up.

Basically, you trim away the blue hair on the body with the clippers, then clip the neck and chest, then the hindquarters (from the tail to below the ankle), leaving the hair on the front of the hind legs. You will trim the tan on the underside of the dog (with the longer hair towards the front of the dog). You also will trim around the feet. On the face, you will trim the bangs with the scissors, trim around the ears and then layer the hair around the face. You might opt to leave the facial furnishings full and top the head with a bow.

The topknot can be formed on the Yorkie's head

once he's five or six months old, when the head furnishings are long enough. With a comb, take a section of hair from above the eyes and near the outside corners and fasten it with a barrette or rubber band. An experienced breeder can show you how to do this correctly. A nice red bow will look great atop the topknot.

If you have grooming problems, you can take your dog to the professional groomer the first time or two for his grooming. The groomer will "set" the pattern and then it will be easier for you to get the Yorkie look by following the pattern that has already been set in the coat. Of course, you can eliminate all of the grooming for yourself, except for the weekly brushing, if you take your dog to the groomer every few months!

If the coat totally grows out before you start to groom, the pattern will be lost and then you will have

A fully groomed Yorkie with a jaunty red bow.

to start over again. Just remember: many pet owners can do just as good, or an even better, job trimming their dogs than

The pet trim is an adorable option for those who do not wish to maintain the full coat. It is also called the "puppy trim," and it's easy to see why.

some professional groomers! Regardless, if you do not keep your dog combed and brushed out, you will have a mess of tangles in no time.

Professional groomers have now started doing the "Miniature Schnauzer" trim on the pet Yorkshire. This will give your dog a short coat that will be easy to keep up and it will surely give him a very cute look.

An old pro at his pedicures, this Yorkie sits politely on the table to have his nails trimmed.

Maintenance on this trim will be very easy, and you should consider it.

It is important to trim your dog's toenails; it is best to start this within a week of bringing him home. Purchase a quality toenail trimmer for pets. You may want to purchase a styptic stick in case you trim the nail too short and bleeding starts. With the Yorkshire Terrier who typically has black toenails, it is difficult to see the blood vessel that runs inside the nail. Until you are familiar with trimming the nails, you may nick it. If you do not start

In the beginning stages of nail clipping, holding the dog on your lap may reassure him.

trimming the nails at a young age, so your dog is used to this, you will have greater difficulty in trimming the nails of an adult who resists his pedicures.

Give your Yorkie at least a weekly brushing, trim his toenails every month or so and give him a bath when he needs it. Consider taking him to the groomer for a cute, easy-to-keep trim. In whatever coat you decide, you will have a good-looking Yorkie in all his delicate beauty.

The delicate beauty of this magnificently coated toy terrier is what attracts many to the breed.

GROOMING YOUR YORKIE

Overview

- It goes without saying that a Yorkie owner has a lot of grooming to do!
- Have the basic equipment on hand so you can accustom your Yorkie to grooming in puppyhood.
- Your grooming method will depend on your Yorkie's coat length and how often you want to take him to a professional groomer.
- Regular brushing, once or more weekly, will keep the coat free of mats and tangles.
- Aside from brushing, bathing and trimming, grooming includes care of the nails and overall checks for good skin and coat health.

Keeping the Yorkie Active

L apdogs like Yorkies can excel in many areas other than laps and sofas! Despite their mere 5 pounds, Yorkies can be exceptional in many activities and they thrive on being busy with their owners.

Some Yorkie owners are looking for something challenging, and there are many activities to keep both dog and owner very busy, active and interested. Even though they are small, Yorkies can excel in many activities because of their intelligence and high energy level.

Lapdogs they may be, but Yorkies enjoy time outdoors just like any other dog.

After puppy kindergarten, you may want to work toward a Canine Good Citizen® award. This program, when successfully completed, shows that your dog will mind his manners at home, in public places and with other dogs. This class is available to dogs (pure-bred or otherwise) of any age. It's a fun course and useful for everyday life. There are ten steps, including: accepting a friendly stranger, sitting politely for petting, accepting light grooming and examination from a stranger, walking on a loose lead, coming when called, responding calmly to another dog, responding to distractions, down on command and remaining calm when the owner is out of sight for three minutes. Upon successful completion, your dog will receive an AKC Canine Good Citizen® certificate.

Safe chew toys will keep your Yorkie's mind and teeth occupied while providing dental benefits as he chews.

Conformation showing is popular among Yorkie fanciers. Show dogs require a full grooming prior to their turn in front of the judge.

With the young pup, you will find that he will like to play games with you with his toys. All puppies like to chase balls and maybe even return them to their owners. Playing games with your dog will delight him. Never give him a toy or ball that is small enough for him to swallow as, like a child, he will swallow it and an expensive trip to the veterinarian may follow.

Obedience is a long-established sport at which Yorkies can excel. Obedience trials are held either by themselves or in conjunction with a conformation show. There are many levels to AKC obedience, starting with Novice, whereupon after completion of three passing "legs" the dog will earn a Companion Dog (CD) title. The courses then continue in difficulty, with Open at the next level. A dog earns a Companion Dog Excellent (CD) upon completion of three successful legs in Open. The next class is Utility (UD) which includes off-lead work,

silent hand signals and picking the right dumbbells from a group of dumbbells. Not many dogs reach this level, so it is a major accomplishment for both owner and dog when a Utility Dog title degree is achieved.

Agility, started in England, is a relatively new sport in America. It is very popular and can be easily found at dog shows. Look for the large noisy ring filled with competitors and dogs running the course and excited spectators watching at ringside, joining in with cheers.

Dogs are taught to run a course that includes hurdles, ladders, jumps and a variety of challenges. There are a number of titles in agility, depending upon the obstacles that the dog is able to conquer. AKC defines agility as "The enjoyment of bringing together communication, training, timing, accuracy and just plain fun in

Yorkie handlers enjoy showing off these breathtaking small wonders in the show ring.

the ultimate game for you and your dog." Lots of exercise for both dog and owner, and there is great joy in watching this small dog race through his paces!

The ultimate in titles is the Versatile Companion Dog.

mentioned activities, it is essential to belong to a dog club where there are equipment and facilities for practice. Find a good school in your area and attend a class as a spectator before enrolling. If you like the facility, the instructor and the type of instruction, sign your dog up for the next series of lessons, which will probably be held two times a week with a choice of mornings or evenings.

The Yorkie, with his small agile body, can navigate the agility weave poles with ease.

This is the degree that recognizes those dogs and handlers who have been successful in multiple dog sports. In order to excel at any of the afore-

Canine sports have become so popular with the public that there should be little difficulty in finding a training facility. You will find it a great experience, working with your dog and meeting new people with whom you will have a common interest. This will all take time and interest on your part, and a willing dog working on the other end of the leash.

Yorkshire Terriers have also been known to do well at tracking, and they do particularly well at pet therapy, which consists of taking your dog to a care center (like a nursing home or hospital) for an hour or two once a week so that he can visit and bring companionship and comfort to the people there.

Of course, the easiest way to keep your dog active and fit is to take him for a walk every morning and evening. This will be good for you, too! Remember that the Yorkshire Terrier is a high-energy dog and he will need lots of activity to keep him a happy camper. Don't expect him to sit around and spend every evening watching television, as he will much prefer to spend some time working with you in an agility class or obedience class, or just going for a nice walk.

KEEPING THE YORKIE ACTIVE

Overview

- He may be small, but he's got lots of energy! The Yorkie is quite an athletic lapdog, willing and able to participate in a range of activities.
- The best type of activity for a Yorkie is done with his beloved owner.
- Look into canine activities like Good Citizen certification, obedience and agility. You may even progress to dog sports on a competitive level.
- Involvement in training clubs or classes will keep you and your Yorkie busy with activity and lots of new Yorkie friends.

CHAPTER 13

Your Yorkie and His Vet

One of the first things to do when bringing home your dog is to find a good veterinarian. Your breeder, if from your area, should be able to recommend someone; otherwise, it will be your job to find a clinic that you like.

A major consideration for finding a veterinarian is to find someone conveniently situated within 10 miles of your home. Find a veterinarian whom you like and trust. You must be confident that he knows what he is doing and is experienced with toy dogs. See that the office looks and smells clean. It is

A healthy Yorkie is a happy Yorkie, jumping for joy at the good care his owner gives him.

your right to check on fees before setting up an appointment, and you will usually need an appointment. If you have a satisfactory visit, take the business card so that you have the clinic's number and the name of the veterinarian you saw. Try and see the same vet at each visit, as he then will personally know the history of your dog and your dog will be familiar with him.

The importance of dental care cannot be stressed enough with a toy breed like the Yorkie.

Inquire if the clinic takes emergency calls and, if they do not, as many no longer do, get the name, address and telephone number of the emergency veterinary service in your area. Keep this handy with your veterinarian's phone number.

On your first visit, take along the documentation that your breeder gave you with a record of the shots that your puppy has had so that the veterinarian will know which series of shots your pup should be getting. You should also take in a fecal sample

Don't forget the other end! The dog's rear should be kept clean and his anal sacs expressed if needed, a job best done by the vet.

for a worm test. Make sure your vet is aware from the outset that some Yorkies can be sensitive to anesthesia.

VACCINES

The vaccines recommended by the American Veterinary Medical Association are called CORE vaccines, those which protect against diseases most dangerous to your puppy and adult dog. These include: distemper (canine distemper virus, CDV), fatal in puppies; canine parvovirus (CPV or parvo), highly contagious and also fatal in puppies and at-risk dogs; canine adenovirus (CAV2), highly contagious and high risk for pups under 16 weeks of age; canine hepatitis (CA1), highly contagious, pups at high risk. These are generally combined into what is often called a five-way shot. Rabies immunization is required in all 50 states, with the vaccine given three weeks after the complete series of the puppy shots.

Non-CORE vaccines no longer routinely recommended by the AVMA, except when the risk is present, are canine parainfluenza, leptospirosis, canine coronavirus, *Bordetella* (canine cough) and Lyme disease (borreliosis). Your veterinarian will alert you if there is any risk of these non-fatal diseases in your town or neighborhood so you can have your dog immunized accordingly.

The American Animal Hospital Association (AAHA) guidelines recommend vaccinating adult dogs every three years instead of annually. Research suggests that annual vaccinations may actually be over-vaccinating and may be responsible for many of today's canine health problems.

Mindful of that, the revised AAHA guidelines on vaccinations also strongly suggest that veterinarians and owners consider a dog's individual needs and exposure before they decide on a vaccine protocol. Many dog owners now have annual titer tests done to check their dog's antibodies rather than automatically vaccinate for parvo or distemper.

Owners should have a basic understanding of all of the diseases for which their dogs are vaccinated. Distemper, at one time, was the scourge of dog breeding, but with the proper immunization and a clean puppy-rearing area, this no longer presents a problem to the reputable breeder. Canine hepatitis, very rare in the United States, is a severe liver infection caused by a virus. Leptospirosis is an uncommon disease that affects the kidneys; it is rare in young puppies, occurring primarily in adult dogs. Parvovirus is recognized by fever, vomiting and diarrhea. This is a deadly disease for pups and can spread very easily through their feces. The vaccine is

highly effective in the prevention of parvovirus.

HEALTH CONCERNS IN THE YORKIE

The Yorkshire Terrier is, overall, a very healthy dog, but

there are a few problems within the breed that you should be aware of. A disorder that can occur in the Yorkshire Terrier is Legg-Calve-Perthes disease (also called Perthes). This is a bone-related disease and not a hereditary disease. It is thought to be caused by an injury or possibly a nutritional

Your vet will manage all details of your pup's vaccination program, picking up where the breeder left off.

problem. The disease appears between four and ten months of age and is very painful. The dog will limp on one or both rear legs and eventually the leg muscles become wasted. There are some treatments for Perthes and these should be discussed with your vet.

Patellar luxation, dislocation of the kneecap, is a skeletal disorder, and reputable breeders will do their best to eliminate it through careful breeding. This defect is caused by poor angulation in the hind legs and lack of musculature as well as by jumping. Owners should limit the amount of jumping that their Yorkies do. Slipped stifles and some spinal cord problems can also be seen in the breed.

Eye problems are not common in the breed, but breeders have begun to pay attention to incidences of progressive retinal atrophy (PRA), hereditary cataracts (HC), keratitis sicca and

distichiasis. Responsible breeders will screen their stock for PRA and HC before breeding.

Health guarantees are important, and a responsible breeder will give you a contract that will guarantee your pup against certain congenital defects. This guarantee will be limited in time to six months or one year. If there is a problem, he will possibly replace the pup or offer some refund in his price.

GOOD HYGIENE

Let's not overlook the usual "housekeeping" with your new puppy. When your dog is a young pup, you should start getting him used to an examination routine. Each time he is groomed, you should check over his ears, eyes and teeth and anal sacs.

Ears should be checked for dirt or any sign of infection. Take a damp cloth—a soft old washcloth can work quite well—and gently wash the inside of the ear. If you notice any build-up of wax or a putrid smell, you should take your dog to the veterinarian to have the ears properly cleaned. If there is an

If you see your dog shaking his head from side to side, holding his head lopsided, scratching at his ear or pushing his head and ear along the carpet or sides of

Belly up! The skin on the tummy should be pink and clean, with no signs of rash or other problems.

infection, the vet will prescribe an ointment or liquid to clear up the problem. Dogs with upright ears, like Yorkies, have more of a chance of getting dirt into the ears, whereas dogs with drop ears have "warm" ears where infections can grow much more easily.

the furniture, you can be almost certain that an ear infection is in the making. Your vet can prescribe a medicated ear solution to treat the infection, and you must be diligent about administering the medication as directed and for the full course of treatment.

CHAPTER 13

When grooming, take your damp washcloth and gently wash the areas around the eyes. Tear staining may occur, or debris can get caught in the coat around the eyes. Warm water or a cleansing solution made for this purpose can be used.

All dogs should have their eyes checked if any redness appears. Quite often you can purchase an over-the-counter medication at the pet shop to clear up the redness. If an eye problem persists, you will have to see your veterinarian.

Toy dogs are infamous for having less than perfect teeth. Start inspecting the teeth regularly when your Yorkie is still a puppy. Teeth should also be brushed on a regular basis. You can clean your dog's teeth yourself by using a piece of washcloth or a piece of gauze, wrapped around your finger. Gently rub your finger back and forth across the teeth as you would a toothbrush. Do not use human toothpaste, but you will find "doggy" toothpaste available if you wish to use it.

If you allow plaque to build up, your dog will have as many dental problems as you would have. Veterinarians will clean your dog's teeth but it is a costly process and does not need to be done by a professional if you have done your work at home. Giving your dog several dog biscuits a day, plus his dry kibble, will help prevent the buildup of plaque.

As a dog ages, as in humans, his gums may recede and he will have further problems and smelly breath. Your vet may tell you that it is necessary to remove one or more teeth, but most dogs continue to eat even if all of their teeth have been pulled. Of course, their diet will be a bit different, but they will fare just as well. A distinctly unpleasant odor from the mouth is a signal that all is not well with your dog's gums or teeth. Early tooth loss, unfortunately, is common in the Yorkshire Terrier, so do your best to ensure your pet's teeth for as long as possible.

All dogs have anal sacs located on either side of the rectum. The contents, very smelly, are used to mark the dog's territory and are usually released when the dog defecates. Occasionally these will have to be expressed by hand. Have your veterinarian show you how to do this the first time and then you can do it at home, even though it is a rather smelly and unpleasant job! A sign that the anal glands are clogged is when your dog scoots across the floor on his fanny. On occasion, the glands will appear swollen, which can be seen on a trimmed Yorkie but is more difficult to notice under the long coat.

The eyes, ears, teeth and anal glands are parts of the general housekeeping of a dog. Start your dog on his cleaning routine at a very early age, doing a bit at a time, and when your dog is an adult you will have little difficulty in performing these preventative-maintenance functions.

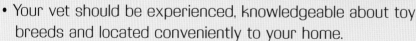

YOUR YORKIE AND HIS VET

Overview

- Your vet should be experienced, knowledgeable about toy breeds and located conveniently to your home.
- Choose a vet with whom you and your Yorkie are comfortable.
- Discuss with your vet the course of inoculations that your puppy is receiving.
- Acquaint yourself with the health problems specific to the breed; your vet should be aware of these, too. Breeders should breed only from genetically healthy dogs.
- Preventative care on your part at home will minimize illness and keep your Yorkie in overall good condition.

Your Aging Yorkie

Yorkie owners are blessed with long-lived dogs who remain hardy and alert well into their double digits.

One of the longest-lived of domestic dogs, the Yorkshire Terrier leads an active life for most of his 14 to 16 years. Owners will notice that the dog starts to slow down as he gets into his teen years. He will not play as hard or as long as he used to and he will sleep more. He will find the sunbeam in the morning hours and take a long nap. At this time, you will probably put him on a senior dog food. Continue to watch his weight, as it is more important than ever not to let your senior citizen become obese. You will notice that his muzzle will become gray and you may see opacities in his eyes, signs of cataracts. And as he becomes older, he may become arthritic.

Continue your walks, making them shorter, and give him a baby aspirin when he appears to be stiff. Talk to your vet about new arthritis medicine that is available for dogs. Keep the grooming up, as both of you will like to have him looking and smelling good. Watch for lumps and bumps and take him to the veterinarian if you notice anything abnormal. Incontinence can also become a problem with the older dog. This is frustrating for you and hard on the house, but he hasn't become "unhousebroken"; rather, it is that his excretory muscle tone is fading.

Veterinary care has changed much over the last decade or two, as has medical care for humans. Your veterinarian can now do much to extend

Caring for a senior dog means more frequent trips to the vet, as changes requiring medical attention can happen quickly.

Two dogs help keep each other active and youthful.

CHAPTER 14

your dog's life if you want to spend the money. Unfortunately, this will extend his life but it will not bring back his youth. Your primary concern should be to help your animal live out his life comfortably, and there are medications that can be helpful for this goal. Whatever you decide, try to put your dog and his well-being and comfort ahead of your emotions and do what will be best for your pet.

Always remember the many wonderful years that your pet gave to you and your family and, with that thought, it may not be long before you are looking for a new puppy for the household. And there you are, back at the beginning with a cute bundle of joy, ready for another 15 years of happiness!

YOUR AGING YORKIE

Overview

- The Yorkshire Terrier has an average lifespan of about 14-16 years. Telltale signs of aging include graying around the muzzle and an overall decrease in activity level.
- Keep giving your Yorkshire Terrier the same good care, making accommodations for his older age.
- A senior dog benefits from more frequent trips to the vet, as early detection of any problems is important.
- Discuss with your vet how to adjust your senior's home-care routine and ask about advances in canine medicine that may benefit your aging friend.
- Remember all of the joy that your Yorkshire Terrier has given you during his life and do all you can to help him live out his senior years as happily and comfortably as possible.